Options Trading

A Beginner's Guide to Earning Passive Income from Home with Options Trading

T. Whitmore

Copyright © 2016 by T. Whitmore All Right Reserved.

No part of this publication may be reproduced, distributed, or transmitted in any form or by any means, including photocopying, recording, or other electronic or mechanical methods, or by any information storage and retrieval system without the prior written permission of the publisher, except in the case of very brief quotations embodied in critical reviews and certain other noncommercial uses permitted by copyright law.

Table of Contents

Options Trading

A Beginner's Guide to Earning

Introduction

DAY 1 Options Essentials

   What is an Option?

DAY 2 Types of Options

   Index Options

   Commodity Options

   Forex Options

   Binary Options

DAY 3 Trading Options

   Placing the Order

   Market Order or Limit Order

   Time Restrictions

DAY 4 Option Pricing

   Pricing Basics

Greeks

   Delta

   Gamma

   Theta

    Vega

Day 5 Buying Selling, Exercising Options

DAY 6 Option Strategies

    Writing Covered Calls

    Selling Naked Puts

    Vertical Spreads

    Calendar Spreads

    Iron Condor

Conclusion

Introduction

In the world of financial trading, options stand alone. It is easy to understand how you can buy and sell shares in the company. It is a slight stretch to understand how you can "short" the things you are trading, selling them before you buy them to make a profit from a reduction in price.

Moving on to derivatives other than options, even these are straightforward.

Things you can buy "deriving" their value from other things, as for example the value of a futures contract changing as the price of the underlying commodity varies, that can be worked with.

But when you get to options trading, while the basic definition is simple the complexity is multiplied. No longer are you looking at a stock which may go say from $51 to $57, thereby simply giving you a profit (or loss) from a $6 move. You are looking at the same stock for which you can pick an option at a price of $45, $50, $55, $60, etc. You also get to pick the date by when you expect the price change to happen. And whether you are bullish or bearish, you can back up your hunch by either buying options, at a cost, or selling them and getting some in- come, though often at a risk as you will see.

This Guide to Options is designed to steer you in the right direction, giving you a full understanding of the many different ways in which you can set up your option trading, and the associated risks and rewards.

I would not advise you to go ahead into options trading on the basis of the information in this book alone. You will however understand the possibilities, and be able to look into the strategies that appeal to you. Unlike some of the entrepreneurs rushing out there, I take the time to explain the basics of what you need to know, so you are in a situation to evaluate any further education and experience you may need.

I hope you're not disappointed to find that reading this book alone will not equip you completely for the task, but you must understand that financial trading of any type takes study and work to perform successfully. One idea that you must keep in mind is that on a trading timescale, which is typically days or weeks, you will not see much fundamental shift in the value of most things. So trading profit comes mainly from other traders' losses.

This is clear when trading something like shares, but equally true with derivatives and options. When you take off the commission that your broker or dealer gets in some manner from your trading, you can see that there is less money to go around, and in fact the majority of traders lose. Therefore you have to educate yourself and trade more smartly than the majority of traders to survive and thrive.

Though the basics of trading are (relatively) immutable, you should consider this book simply the start of your option trading education and career. It is my intent to give you the best grounding possible, so that you can look forward to a long and successful vocation.

DAY 1 Options Essentials

What is an Option?

What is an Option?

An option is a guarantee that provides you the right, to either go long or go short on the underlying futures contract at a pre-determined entry price on or before a specific date. Each offers the opportunity to take advantage of price moves in the futures markets without actually having a futures position. Options are available for each futures contract delivery month for up to two years into the future.

There are two types of options, call options and put options. Call and put options are separate option contracts. They are not the opposite side of the same contract. For every call client there is a call agent, and for every put buyer, there is a put seller. The buyer pays a premium to the seller in each transaction.

Call Option

The call option grants the buyer the right, but not the obligation, to go deep on the underlying products futures contract at a pre-specified entry price (i.e., strike price) on or ahead of an expiration date. You would usually buy a call option when you believe that the futures value will grow.

Put Option

A put option provides the purchaser the power, but not the responsibility, to go short on the underlying stock futures agreement at a pre-specified entry cost on or ahead of a particular date. A put option is employed when you consider the futures price will reduce.

Option Buyer

The buyer or holder of an option can choose to exercise their right to hold onto the option until it mature, trade it before it expires, or simply let the option expire.

Option Seller

An options seller is also called the writer. The seller is usually a speculator and is obligated to take the opposite futures position if the buyer exercises their right. In return for the premium, the seller assumes the risk of taking an adverse position.

There are many different types of options when trading depending when, where and who you are trading with. However to understand the basics and get a real grasp on this kind of investing we will keep it simple.

Let us begin with the American option.

American Option - Can be employed at any moment between the time of buying and the expiration date. Most exchange-traded are of this kind.

European Option - The only difference a European option and an American version is that they can only be exercised at the time of the expiration date.

The strange thing is that the American and European moniker have nothing to do with geographical location. It is the just the terms used to distinguish between the two different types.

I'm afraid options get even more complicated. Now we need to look at the other types out there starting with long-term options.

Long- Term Options

When people think about options trading they often only consider short-term options of a couple of months or so. It is possible to have options that can be held for years for long-term investors.

At this point in the financial world, they become what we know as LEAPS (long-term equity anticipation securities). They are the same as short-term options except they offer opportunities over a longer period. LEAPS aren't available on every stock but are still readily available on the most widely held issues.

Exotic Options and Plain Vanilla Options

The initial call and puts options are sometimes called "plain vanilla." Don't be scared they are easy enough to follow.

A plain vanilla option is a standard option type. Having a simple expiration date and strike price, and that is it. With an exotic option, there may be other contingencies such as a knock-on options that become active when the stock hits a pre-determined price point. In other words...

Because of the versatility of options; there exist many types and variations. Non-standard options are called exotic options. These are either variation on the payoff profiles of the plain vanilla option or are wholly different products with "optionality" embedded in them.

Look this is a complex subject at times and it took me time to get to grips with the whole options trading ethos. All I can stress is until you are completely confident that you understand the intricacies of options trading, don't invest as you could lose a lot of money.

The following are ordinarily employed in the options trading process.

Strike Price

The strike price, also known as the exercise price, is the price at which an option holder - the buyer - may enter the underlying futures contract if they use the option. For call options, the strike price is the entry price at which one has the right to go long on the underlying commodity futures contract. For put options, this is the entry price at which one has the right to go short on the product.

Underlying Futures Contract

The fair futures contract that may be acquired or sold upon the exercise of the option. For example, an option on the December Silver futures contract is the right to buy or sell one December Silver futures contract.

Premium

The premium is a market-determined price (cost) of the option (which does not include commission and fees) that the buyer pays to purchase either a call option or a put option. It is a non-refundable cost that the option seller keeps, and is your maximum amount of risk in the market. Depending on your motive for purchasing the option, the premium represents either the cost of price protection (as a hedger) from adverse price movement, or the cost of opportunity (as a speculator) to profit potentially from a welcome price move with a pre-defined risk amount.

The option premium is quoted just like the price of the underlying futures contract; in cents, points, etc., but in some instances, the value of a "tick", or point, is different than the underlying futures contract.

Option premiums fluctuate daily due to market conditions. Just like with futures contracts, you profit if you first buy a call option at a particular premium (price), and then sell it back to the market at a higher price. If you monitor changes in an option's premium for at least two weeks, you may be able to buy your option at a reduced price.

Professional traders use various statistical analysis to compute what an option's premium should be. However, actual option premiums are determined through competitive bidding at the Exchange. Factors that determine the premium include:

* The current price of the underlying futures contract

* The volatility of the underlying futures contract

* The strike price concerning the current price of the underlying futures contract

* The amount of time remaining before the option expires

* Interest rates

For call options, the closer the strike price is to the underlying futures price, the more expensive the option is. For puts, the closer the strike price is to the futures price; the higher the option will be.

Options have two separate components that together define the option's premium. Exercising an option into the underlying futures contract will require you to post margin for the position, and you will also incur an additional cost from the commission to open the futures position.

Expiration Date

All options are assigned an expiration date after which they are no longer valid for trading purposes. This is the last day that the option may be exercised. Frequently, this date will be 2-4 weeks before the underlying futures contract's Last Trading Day (LTD), although some futures items synchronize the option expiration date with the futures contract LTD.

The farther out into the future an option's expiration date is, the more expensive the option will be (time = money). Any time before the option expiration date, an option purchaser can either exercise the option. (i.e., convert it to the underlying futures contract. this is at the strike price of the option being the entry point of the futures contract), liquidate the option (i.e., sell it back to the market), or let it expire worthless. You would only exercise an option if it were in-the-money (that is, the option is profitable). Option speculators rarely use their option. Instead, they will liquidate the option to either take profit when it has increased in value, or to prevent further time value loss (especially for expensive options).

If the option is either not exercised or liquidated by the option expiration date, and the option is not in-the-money, it will automatically expire worthless. If an option expires worthless, only the option seller benefits from the trade because they receive the full premium of the option when it was sold. The expired option also lets the option seller get out of their short option position without the need to initiate an offsetting transaction. In contrast, the seller of a futures contract can only get out of their position by offsetting it with another purchase or making delivery on the contract.

Automatic Exercise.

At the close of the option's expiration date, all in-the-money options are automatically exercised by BOT Clearinghouse. This means if the option you purchased is in-the-money when it expires, it will be converted to the underlying futures contract. If this does happen, make sure you establish a Stop-Loss Order with this futures position! However, it is best not to let this happen by liquidating the option a few weeks before the expiration date. So in summary, you buy either a call or put option to acquire it, and you liquidate your option to relinquish control of it.

Volatility

Volatility is a measure of how fast and how much the futures price changes and is expressed as a percentage - without regard to direction. It is considered the most important factors in selecting options for trading. Option prices become expensive when volatility is high (i.e., price movement is quick, and there are substantial changes in price magnitude). Conversely, option prices are less high when futures prices are quiet, and the market is not moving very much. The higher the volatility of a market, the more expensive an option will be.

An option with three months to expiration might command a higher premium in a volatile market than an option with six months to expiration in a stable market. Of the different ways to measure volatility, the two most important are implied volatility and statistical volatility.

* Implied volatility is used to determine the current market price of an option.

It uses the Black-Scholes formula to translate option premium into an accurate assessment of what traders "expect" the market to do. Also, it is a measure of trader sentiment. Option prices are affected most by changes in the underlying futures contract price, and second by changes in trader sentiment.

* Statistical volatility (also called historic volatility) is a description of real price alters during a distinct time in the past.

Day Order

By default (and unless you stipulate otherwise), all orders you give to your broker are day orders. This means that if you place an order without any of the specifications described below, your order will apply for only that trading day. Each of the following orders may be submitted as a day order, or with other specified conditions. A common overriding condition available to traders is the good until canceled (also called 'GTC') order. When you specify GTC with your order, you are saying, "I want this order to continue from today onwards, until my order is either filled or I call my broker and cancel the order." Note: if you do GTC place orders, be certain you write it down, so you don't forget they exist. This will help you avoid unpleasant surprises when a forgotten order is filled - but the market's now going.

Stop Order

This is an order to buy at a price higher than the current market price, or to sell at a cost lower than the current market price. Stop orders may be used to buy into an up trending market or close your position in a down trending market. The stop order becomes a market order when the stop price is reached (touched). A stop order can be used as a risk management tool to protect open options. If price moves unfavorably (to the stop price), the stop order is executed, and the option position is liquidated, preventing any further loss of the option position.

Market-If-Touched Order

This order lets you buy at a price below the current market price or sell at a price higher than the current market price. When the specified price is "touched," in the opposite direction! This order becomes a market order. This order can only be placed on certain exchanges.

Market-On-Close Order

This order may only be executed in the closing price range at the close of the trading day. This order is not available for all products.

Cancel/Replace Order

This order cancels out a previously entered order and replaces it with a new order.

Long Option

A long option is one that you buy. It can either be a long call or a long put. This is a limited risk option trade.

Short Option

A short option is one that you sell. It can either be a short call or a short put. This is an option trade with a risk that is not limited.

DAY 2 Types of Options

Index Options

Option trading is not restricted to individual stocks. The large commodity market is an option market that deals in all manners of commodities such as grain or cattle. There is also another type of investment known as index option trading.

An index is a listing of some different stocks that share something in common, and it represents the composite value of all of them. An example is the Dow Jones Industrial Average which represents the value of the 30 largest and most widely held industrial stocks on the New York Stock Exchange. The Pattern and Poor's 500 is a different index that represents 500 different stocks. These two well-known indices are frequently used to gauge the progress of the economy and the general health of the stock market. They are familiar to most people, even those with little or no interest in the market, as they are widely quoted on news broadcasts.

They represent just two of a large number. There are broad-based ones that reflect a wide range of widely different stocks, and there are ones that are very specific to a particular group. As the Dow Jones tracks industrial stocks, another index called The Morgan Stanley Biotech Index tracks 36 different stocks of companies engaged in biotech research. An index can list firms with similar goods, and even similar management styles. There are also a wide variety of foreign indices that reflect the composite value of foreign stocks.

An index may also be classified as to how it is weighted. Some regard every stock equally, and a price fluctuation in any stock in the index will have an impact on the index price no matter how large that individual stock's share of the index might be. Other indices "weight" the index based on the size of the company. In other words, small enterprises that experience even a large price change will not have as much impact on the index as a slight change in one of the most significant companies.

Index option trading is widespread in part because the risk is considered to be lower than with individual stock. This is partly because the index, representing a variety of stocks, is less likely to be subjected to the same adverse pressures that may cause an individual company to experience a very rapid decline in its value. The index is seen as much easier to subject to trend analysis, and this makes it an attractive part of most Mutual Fund portfolios.

There is another classification of indices that might be of interest to investors with certain social and environmental sensitivities. They are known as Ethical Indices as list stocks that satisfy certain criteria in their business operation. An example of one such index is the Wilderhill Clean Energy Index. Sadly, in the current market there is no direct connection between environmental sensitivity and profit, but with an Ethical Index, you can at least feel good about yourself while you make money, or even feel somewhat good if your investment turns out the opposite way.

Among the many investment opportunities that exist, option trading stands as both one of the most exciting and risky as well as one that offers some of the best chances for a substantial return. Learn all about options basics, stock and options trading, options strategies, and options pricing at http://www.option-trading-fortune.com

Commodity Options

Just like stock options, commodity option trading gives the investor the obligation to purchase or sell an underlying asset at a set value during a particular period. But in the case of commodity option trading, the underlying asset isn't stock, but a commodity.

A commodity is something more substantial than a stock; it is an actual product. Goods considered to be commodities are those that come up out of the earth and are in their raw, unprocessed form. Examples of products are things like wheat, oil, coffee and gold. All of these things have a value determined by the market, which is of coursed based on supply and demand. Most of us know that oil is a valuable commodity, and its value is likely to stay high unless we discover a new, cheaper source of energy to run our vehicles. Many commodities, however, can have much bigger fluctuations in price, which makes them an excellent investment opportunity.

Commodity option trading is a way for investors to be able to make a profit on the changeable value of products without massive investments or risk. An investor purchases the right to buy or sell the underlying commodity at the strike price within a given period. A profit can be made if the change in the value is enough to cover the premium paid for the option; if the change that is anticipated doesn't occur, the investor loses the premium.

Commodity option trading follows many of the same rules as stock options and has the same two basic types of transaction, the call, and the put. The call allows the holder of the option to buy the underlying asset at the strike price, while a put allows the option buyer to sell at the strike price.

Because the option is being purchased on goods that often don't exist yet - such as a harvest of wheat, it is often referred to as futures trading. Commodities can be very volatile - as can stocks, and it carries risks to the investor. Knowledge of the commodity market is vital to successful investing in this area.

Commodity option trading, like all the possibilities, is less risky than outright purchase of a product and requires a smaller investment. This makes it a great way for the average investor to get into the products market even if they don't have a lot of money with which to invest.

Forex Options

Option trading which is commonly associated with stock trading is popular in forex market too. There are two types of forex option trading. These are:

a) Call/ Put option, which operates just like the respective stock option.

B) SPOT or single payment option trading which offers greater flexibility to forex traders.

Call / Put or the traditional Options

In call / put forex option trading the buyer has a right to buy but not the obligation to purchase something from the option seller at a predetermined price and time. To quote an example, a trader might purchase an option to buy three lots of EUR/USD at 1.4000 in a month. This contract in forex terminology is known as an "EUR call/USD put." In case the price of EUR/USD falls to less than 1.4000, the option expires without the buyer NIL any amount. The buyer will only lose the premium amount. However, if EUR/USD increases to 1.5000, then the buyer can exercise his option and gain three lots of EUR/USD for only 1.4000. He can, in turn, sell these for a profit in the market.

FOREX options are traded over the counter. The traders can, therefore, pick the price and date on which the option is to be valid. There are two types of Call/put options American Style and European style.

Single Payment Options Trading (SPOT)

In SPOT forex option trading, the trader enters a scenario and lets it play out. To quote an example "EUR/USD will break 1.400 in 10 days will be input by the trader. He will obtain a premium quote also known as the option cost quote. If EUR/USD breaks 1.400, he will receive a payout.

Primarily in SPOT forex options, if the trader is right he accepts cash into his account. If not, he loses his premium. A distinct advantage of SPOT is that it allows a choice of scenarios. The actual decision is left to the trader depending upon his prediction of the market behavior.

In SPOT your option is automatically converted into cash when your option trade is thriving resulting receipt of a payout. One significant disadvantage of SPOT options is greater premiums compared to standard options.

Depending upon your unique needs you can choose the type of forex option trading you wish to engage in.

Forex market trading is no longer the domain of large institutions alone. Ordinary individuals like you and me can readily learn the basics of forex trading education and start trading profitably in the market.

Binary Options
Getting Started

Most trading platforms give two mild choices when it comes to binary trading: a put option and a call option. The put option is preferred if the trader considers that the price will decrease, while the call option is available for if they suppose that the price will rise. All traders need to decide their position based on any number of market factors, and numerous trading methods and algorithms can be used, which will be covered later.

Before choosing your position, you will be required to choose a trading platform through which you will be conducting all of your trades. Choosing the right broker to handle your finances is vital to the success of your trades, especially for beginning traders who need to make the most of all financial options. Not all brokers will be able to provide you with the same methods of trading, just like not all brokers will have the same limitations and returns available on their websites. For beginning traders, it is recommended not to worry about some of the more complicated binary trading methods. For now, choose a good brokerage that offers a high percentage of their returns, and see if there are any incentive programs offered that you can take advantage of.

Tips to Keep Remember

As with everything, there are various tips and tricks that beginning traders can keep in mind to increase their chances of profiting. Many of these tips are also designed to allow individuals to enjoy a much more comfortable trading experience, especially if they need a few rules of thumb to keep in mind as they trade. Eventually, as the trader becomes more and more experienced, they will be able to develop their trading methods and attitudes, designed specifically to complement their unique approach to trading. For now, however, just remembering a few of these simple tips can be enough to help most traders get a head start.

Leave Emotions Out of Your Trades

Perhaps the most important piece of advice to remember is never to rely on gut feelings or intuitive expectations. Trading binary options is not like gambling or any other mere money making process. While chance still plays a role in determining your profits, the vast majority of them will be determined by carefully analyzed indicators and effectively implemented strategies. Traders who rely on their instincts or any emotional connections with their finances will find that they will begin losing money in the long term, no matter what accidental profits they may secure at first.

Making emotionally driven trades is a vast mistake that, unfortunately, many entry level traders make. If your head is not clear and you are not thinking rationally, you will end up making trading mistakes. It is as simple as that. If you begin to feel frustrated or angry with your trades or become too excited after successful ones, it is important to take a step back, take a deep breath, and think about taking a break.

Think About Yourself as a Trader

The most prosperous traders are the individuals who know themselves and know what they want to get out of their trades. These are people who have looked into different types of options and have chosen to work with ones that match their personalities as traders. Most trades can be defined by the short, medium, and long term. Short term trades are identified by very quick transactions that take place in volatile environments, such as sixty-second and two-minute trades. Medium term trades refer to any transactions that can be made between five and fifteen minutes. Long term trades, as the name suggests, represent longer expiry periods, which can range anywhere from an hour to a day, depending on the broker.

As you can tell from the range, there is an approach to each type, one that helps define the trader. If you thrive in fast-paced situations and enjoy the risks that come with dealing with volatility, you will be better suited to work with short term trades. On the other hand, if you enjoy a lower degree of risk and plan on trading steadily for the long term, you may benefit from longer expiry options. Understanding your level of comfort and moving with it is crucial for all traders.

Start Slow

No matter how you plan on approaching the field, it is crucial for you to take your time and become familiar with your chosen strategy. Always start slow and become comfortable with your trading before you increase the size of your trades. Not only is this important in determining the success of your trades, but it can also help you make better decisions when it comes to different market situations. Whenever you have the chance, it is recommended for you to practice with some demo software to make sure that you know how to work with your strategy.

Analyze every trade you make and determine why they were successful or not. Just by reviewing your trades, you will be able to make much better decisions in the future. The more time that you are willing to spend analyzing your trades, the more successful you will be. The measure of a good trader is not in the sheer number of successful trades that they have made, but in their willingness to learn from their mistakes and continue improving.

Limit Your Losses Through Money Management Strategies

Everybody experiences a bad streak now and then, but not all traders know how to deal with it. They may end up making further poor decisions as a result, and, before they know it, they will end up losing a significant portion of their finances. Many people are familiar with the saying "Do not put all of your eggs in one basket." This saying applies to a variety of situations and is particularly important for traders to remember as well.

If you find that you are risking too much of your capital behind a single trade, take a step back and evaluate your finances. A good rule of thumb to remember is never to risk more than five percent of your current funds on any one trade. Many traders also strongly recommend taking a break for the day if you lose more than fifteen percent of your finances. No matter what, however, by keeping these money management strategies in mind, and adjusting them accordingly, you will still have a sizable portion of your capital available, even if things go wrong.

Diversify Your Strategies

In most other investment markets, traders will be strongly encouraged to diversify their investments. This is another good money management strategy, as it can allow them to spread their risk more evenly over a wider variety of commodities. It will ensure that they never lose too much of their investment, because where one product may fail, there will be others that are thriving. However, while this strategy may be useful with other types of trading, binary options can benefit from a different kind of diversification.

Binary options traders will be expected to be able to deal with a wide variety of diverse market situations, each of which can affect many commodities at varying times. It is for this reason that, instead of diversifying their assets, binary option traders are encouraged to expand their approaches and strategies. By understanding how different market climates can end up affecting their commodities, they will be able to act appropriately, without having to worry about taking breaks from their trades.

DAY 3 Trading Options

Placing the Order

How to Place An Order

Your broker will help you place your order. It's their job to help you - that's why you pay them a commission.

1. When you place an order, give your broker the following information:

* Your Account Number (if it's not your particular dealer)

* This is an Options order

* Whether you are buying a put option or a call option

* The number of options desired

* The Month and commodity

* The Strike Price

* The type of Order: Market, Limit, Stop, Day, Open, etc.

Unless you state otherwise, all orders given to your broker will be Day Orders and will expire at the completion of the trading day the order was given. No Open Orders are accepted on New York markets.

2. Listen to your broker when they verbally confirm your order. It is your responsibility to confirm that your broker has repeated your order correctly.

3. You must keep a written record of each order you give to your dealer. This will not only help you avoid "forgetting" about a trade, but it also gives you a way to monitor your trading results. A written record of all your trades also offers historic data about your trades which you can analyze for potential improvements you can make to your trading plan. Several forms are included with this trading course to help you track your option trades.

Market Order or Limit Order

Market Order

This order does not put any restriction on the price you are willing to pay (if you are buying) or accept (if you are selling). It is used to get your order filled quickly. It is important to understand that the last option price quoted is only an indication of the prior market and is not necessarily the price you will receive when your market order is filled. The advantage using a market order is that when markets are trading, your order will be filled quickly. The disadvantage is that, in a highly volatile market, your order may be completed at a much higher or lower price than you anticipated.

Limit Order

This order lets you buy at a price lower than the current market price or to sell at a price higher than the current market price. This order is particularly useful if you are trying to stay within a certain price trading range. Limit orders are executed at the limit price, but if your order is filled, you are guaranteed that price or better. The disadvantage of the limit order is that your price may not be hit, and you may miss the market move. By default, the limit order is a day order (i.e., it only applies for that trading day) unless you specify other conditions (i.e., good until canceled, which means the order stands until it is either filled or canceled)

Time Restrictions

Time Restrictions refers to the amount of time remaining before the option expires. The likelihood of an option becoming profitable depends on the amount of time remaining until the option expires. The longer an option has until expiration, the more expensive it will be. This is because the underlying market has more time for the price to move, with a greater probability of moving substantially in one direction or another. Time value is a non-linear, decaying component of an option's value, so the loss of the option's time value will increasingly accelerate as time approaches the option's expiration date. This causes the value of the option to rapidly erode with the onset of the expiration date because the likelihood of a significant move occurring before expiration decreases. It's a good idea to liquidate expensive options three to four weeks before the option's expiration date to avoid the sharp time value loss.

DAY 4 Option Pricing

Pricing Basics

This chapter describes the technical aspects of option price behavior.

Greeks

The term Greeks is used to describe specific data values which are used by professional traders to analyze options. Top option traders know how changes in the Greeks will affect the profitability of their trades and adjust their trades accordingly. This information will help you define the risk of an option trade. The expected profit or loss of an option is based on changes in market price, time until expiration, as well as changes in implied option volatility.

Here is an example of why the Greeks are important. You purchase an over-priced call option. The futures market price rises steeply, but the value of your call option goes down. This is an example of the implied volatility being drained out of an option. In this case, the reduction in implied volatility (the adverse effect of Vega) was stronger than the price gain expected from market movement (the positive effect of the delta).

This can often happen after a major news event. After the news is out, the implied volatility of the option goes down because the "unknown" becomes" known". When this happens, speculating traders are no longer willing to pay a high premium for the option. Also, option sellers have less exposure to volatility risk, so their asking premium (selling price) also declines. This effect can be even more dramatic in thinly traded markets (i.e., markets with low volume) where few option sellers have greater control of the options market.

Option traders learn early in their career that a change in implied volatility can completely alter the option price. It is best to either buy low volatility, sell it when it's high, or use strategies that can neutralize the effects of this factor. When considering an option trade, you have to make assumptions about what you expect to happen to the Greeks as a trade commences.

Assuming that the implied option volatility or actual statistical volatility of the underlying futures price will stay unchanged is just as important as estimating that it will increase or decrease. Being wrong about this one factor can turn what you believe is a profitable trade into a losing trade. Some markets may exhibit a stable tenancy for implied volatility to increase with directional price moves. For example, implied volatility will increase in the S&P and stock indexes if the futures market price drops. Like-wise, volatility will increase in the grains or the softs if the futures price rallies.

There are several terms used to describe the relationship between the futures price and an option. These terms are referred to as the Greeks and are described below. Note: Except for Delta, the only way to get the Greeks for individual options or option spreads is to use an alternative software program such as OptionVue or from a broker who uses one. Manually calculating these values is too cumbersome.

Delta

Delta tells you how much of a change to expect - either an increase or decrease - in the option's premium when the underlying futures price moves. The projected price change in the option's premium is expressed as a percent of the variation in the price of a full futures contract.

Typically, option premiums do not modify cent-for-cent with shifts in the underlying futures price. This is because options that are in-the-money are more sensitive to changes in the underlying futures price than options that are either at-the-money or out-of-the-money. The price of a deep out-of-the-money option will move at a different magnitude than the price of an at-the-money option for the same price movement of the corresponding futures contract.

The delta value tells you how much the option price will change, percent-wise, when the futures price moves. At-the-money call options will have a delta of 0.50, meaning that you can expect the option to gain 50 percent of what the futures would gain on a price increase. A delta of 1.0 will cause a 1:1 movement between the futures price and the option premium.

However, the delta of an option is not fixed, but changes with variations in the futures price. As the futures price gets closer to the strike price, the value of delta increases. If the option goes in-the-money, the delta value will increase and vice versa. The further in-the-money that the option goes, the larger the delta value will be, causing the change in the option's premium to more closely mirror the change in the futures price.

Delta is continuously positive for calls and adverse for puts. Puts have a negative delta because puts increase in value when the futures price declines. If there is no change in implied volatility, you should expect a market decline to reduce the value of a long call option, just as would the passage of time. For combination positions involving multiple options, use the sum of all the deltas to get the combined delta for the entire position.

How To Calculate Delta

To calculate the delta of an option, you need the futures and option prices from two consecutive days. Calculate the change in the option price (premium) by subtracting yesterday's premium from today's premium. Do the same for the futures price, subtracting yesterday's close from today's close, to find the change in the futures price.

Gamma

The gamma tells you how much the option's delta will change when the underlying futures price changes. As the futures price moves, the delta changes, and gamma can tell you how much change to expect in the delta. If you start out with a delta of 0.50 in a call option, a rally in the underlying futures price will cause delta to increase.

Gamma tells you how much you would expect Delta to change on a 100 point move in the futures. Just as we need to know how much we expect the price of an option to change according to its delta, we need to have an idea of how much the delta itself will change with market movement. Gamma will always be positive if you are a long premium in either calls or puts, and negative if short.

Theta

Theta

This value tells you how much the option's price will decline in one day if the future price does not move at all. It is a reflection of time value loss and is expressed as a dollar amount. Theta is a variable that can be affected either by changes in the futures price, time left until expiration and changes in implied volatility.

All other things being equal, long options decline in value as time passes, and this effect accelerates as time gets closer to the option expiration date. Since any option that is in-the-money has intrinsic value that is equal to its position beyond its strike price, any premium value beyond that is the time premium. Because all time premium will be gone at option expiration, theta tells you how much of that premium you expect to lose on a long option (or gain on a short option) on a daily basis. Options or combination positions which have several months of time value remaining until expiration will have a little premium loss from time decay. The theta value will be positive for short option positions and negative for long positions.

Vega

This value tells you how much the option price will change if implied volatility changes. It is the "sensitivity" of the option's price to volatility. Vega is expressed as a dollar amount. A positive Vega indicates that a rise in implied volatility will benefit your position. Vega tells you how much you can expect the theoretical value of an option to change based on a 1 percent change in implied volatility. For example, if the implied volatility of an option rises from 20 % to 30 %, it has risen 10 percent, regarding calculating the Vega.

However, when comparing the implied volatility of an option that is at 30 percent to one that is trading at 20 percent, the first one has a 50 percent higher implied volatility.

Some facts about the Greeks

All of the Greeks are values which reflect a point in time. Because they are dynamic, they will change with the passage of time, if implied volatility changes. Because the Greeks are "related", if the Delta changes, the Gamma, Theta, and Vega will change too. This trading knowledge and experience can be very helpful in making some important assumptions about how a trade will respond in the future.

Day 5 Buying Selling, Exercising Options

When using options in the stock market, the underlying asset is 100 shares of a specific stock or exchange-traded fund (ETF). Options are also available on some broad-based indexes. When entering an order to buy or sell options, your broker electronically sends the order to one of the option exchanges where the order is executed. This is essentially the same method used to buy or sell stock.

If you ever elect to exercise an option, notify your broker, who takes care of the rest of the process. There is nothing else for the option owner to do – it is an automatic process once you exercise the option. If you trade an option and later are allowed an exercise notice, you are notified about this transaction (it is an operation because when assigned, you either buy or sell stock at the strike price) by your broker.

The notification arrives before the market opens the next trading day. The assignment occurs overnight. If you are designated an exercise notice on a call option, 100 shares will have been removed from your account and replaced with cash (100 * strike price; less commissions) by the time you see your account information on the following business day. It is the same as if you sold 100 shares overnight.

If assigned to a put option, 100 shares appear in your account, and the cash to pay for those shares (plus commissions) has been removed. Again, you bought 100 shares while the markets profit. In other words, there is no notice of a pending assignment. Once you are notified, the assignment is permanent (it cannot be reversed without making a new stock trade to offset the assignment). Most exercises and assignments occur at expiration, but it is possible for an option owner to exercise an option before expiration. It does not happen very often, but there is one exception when a call option is deep in the money.

Sometimes an option is exercised one day before the stock goes ex-dividend. That happens because option owners do not collect dividends. Only stockholders do. Thus, the call owner who wants the dividend must exercise the option and convert it to stock.

DAY 6 Option Strategies

Options are versatile investment tools, and there are many ways to use them. Some methods are highly speculative. Some are conservative. I recommended learning conservative strategies, particularly in the beginning of your option trading career.

Later, if you must, you can attempt more aggressive methods.

I believe that traditional strategies are beneficial in helping the average individual investor earn additional profits from an investment portfolio. Thus, I limit the lessons that I teach to strategies that come with limited risk.

The strategies used most often during my trading career include (additional details below):

-- Writing covered calls

-- Selling naked puts

-- Credit and debit spreads (Vertical spreads)

-- Calendar Spreads

-- Iron Condors

This listing is not exhaustive since there are many more strategies that traders use. This list is suitable for the newer trader. Just know that because of their versatility, options can be combined into very complex strategies used only by professional traders.

Once you understand how a few strategies work, you will have an excellent idea as to the type of policy that best suits your investing objectives, your tolerance for risk, and most importantly, your character traits (i.e., lack of greed and good discipline). However, any lengthy discussion of these strategies is beyond the scope of this book. The short descriptions below are designed to give readers an idea of what can be done with options.

Writing Covered Calls

This involves buying 100 shares of stock and selling one call option. The word 'covered' refers to the fact that when selling any option, there is always the possibility that you will be assigned an exercise notice. As mentioned earlier, when you are assigned an exercise notice on a call option, you are required to deliver (i.e., sell) 100 shares to the person who used.

When you already own the shares, then the call option is 'covered' – meaning that you own the shares, and they can be delivered. When you do not own the shares, then the option is considered to be 'uncovered' or 'naked.' When that happens, you still must deliver the shares. If your account is allowed to sell stock short, then your position will change from being short call options to being short 100 shares of the underlying stock for each call option that was exercised. Most brokers do not allow novice option traders to write (sell) open calls, so you are not expected to run into this problem.

When adopting this strategy, the trader owns a slightly bullish position. The primary risk is that the stock price will decline sharply. No matter what else happens, you, the covered call writer, gets to keep the premium collected from selling the call option (minus your broker's commission). The best possible result is achieved when the stock price increases – giving the trader a capital gain. There is a maximum possible profit, and that occurs when the stock price is higher than the strike price ($85 in this example) when expiration arrives.

When the stock is less than the strike price (and most of the time when it equals the strike price) at expiration, it expires and becomes worthless. You keep your stock and may write another call option with a later expiration date. When the stock is above the strike price at expiration, then the option owner exercises and pays $85 per share. Thus, your profits are capped, or limited. You cannot sell your shares at any price above $85.

Selling Naked Puts

This is about as simple as a strategy can be. However, you must be aware that large losses are possible. Translation: If you would consider buying 200 shares of stock, then it is appropriate to sell two puts because if you are assigned an exercise notice, you would own 200 shares. If you stray from this rule, there will remain the possibility of hurting your trading account. There are two primary plans when selling naked put options:

•The investor is willing to buy a stock at the strike price. Note: The final cost of buying the shares equals the strike price, minus the premium collected from the put sale.

•The trader has no interest in buying stock. He/she is looking to earn a profit from the trade. That is accomplished by closing the position when satisfied with the profit. Sometimes you may seek the maximum possible profit and allow the puts to expire worthless. At other times, the stock price may decline, and you may fear to lose too much money. You solve that dilemma. The best choice is to cover the position and accept a loss (before it becomes a large loss).

Vertical Spreads

This represents an inventive method for selling options – but with reduced risk and reduced profit potential. Why would anyone be willing to make a trade with a smaller maximum benefit? Because the sum that can be lost when an unforeseen event occurs is so significant that it becomes worthwhile to eliminate that possibility in return for accepting less potential gain.

If you accept this idea, then you are already on your way to understanding how to manage risk when trading. It is my hope that the most crucial factor that determines any trader's future success or failure is the trader's ability to manage risk. In that spirit, I recommend adopting strategies with limit risk Calendar Spreads (also known as Time Spreads) The calendar is composed of two options – one bought and the other sold.

Calendar Spreads

The calendar is composed of two options – one bought and the other sold. The underlying asset and the strike price are identical, but the expiration dates are different. The theory is that when the shorter-term option is covered (either by expiring worthless or being purchased in a closing transaction), the trader can sell the longer-term option at a premium that is higher than the original debit paid for the spread. The difference between the purchase and sale price (as with all trades) represents a profit or loss.

How the calendar spread earns a profit:

1. Time decay.

- Options are a wasting asset and when all else remains unchanged, lose value every day.

- Shorter-term options decay more rapidly than longer-term options.

- An option whose strike price is very near that of the underlying stock has more time premium than other options. Translation: When the stock is near the strike price of the calendar spread, the position earns the highest profit.

Iron Condor

This is a fancy name for a simple idea:

- A position consisting of two vertical spreads

- Both spreads use the same underlying asset

- Both spreads expire at the same time (Dec 19, 2014)

- One spread consists of calls (strikes 1250 and 1260)

- One spread consists of puts Strikes 1140 and 1150)

- Both spreads are credit spreads

- Position Objective

Earn money from the passage of time When the iron condor works: As time passes, and INDX remains far away from 1150 and 1250, all options lose value due to time decay. In fact, when enough time passes (expiration arrives) and the options remain out of the money (that means INDX is above 1150 and below 1250) then all four options become worthless. Remember that you sell two vertical spreads when constructing an iron condor, and the cash collected from that sale represents the maximum profit that can be achieved.

Iron Condor Risk: When INDX does not remain comfortable between the strike prices of the options sold (1150 and 1250), then one portion of the iron condor position results in a monetary loss. This is clearly seen in the risk graph. When INDX moves through 1150 on a market decline, or through 1250 on a rally, the value of the options that were sold increases so much – that the trader loses money. [Yes, the put spread becomes almost worthless when INDX moves above 1250, but the loss on the call spread is far greater than the gain on the put spread.] The good news is that risk is limited.

As you will understand when trading options it is important to trade with limited risk and I encourage you to avoid all option positions that come with unlimited risk (selling naked calls, for example). One further point on risk: Having "limited risk" is not enough. You will want to learn all about managing risk so that all positions have an acceptable (to you and your comfort zone) amount of risk and an acceptable potential reward (profit). It takes a bit of experience to get a good feel for how to accomplish that, but please keep in mind that it is easy to make money with options. The problem is that it is also easy to lose money with options and all traders have to avoid losing too much money on any given trade. That is the only way to be assured that losses do not overwhelm profits.

Conclusion

In summary thousands of small retail traders are making a living, and some a fortune, from trading options and you are eager to take a shot at it too, aren't you? So, what are some of the things you must know to master options trading?

What are stocks and shares and how they work?

Stock options are derivatives of shares. This means that you need to know what shares are in the first place to understand the role of options and how options work. In fact, you will need to be a master of stock and shares behavior before you could be a master of options trading because options are merely tools that help you exploit these stock and shares behavior profitably.

What options are

It sounds like common sense but most options traders start out thinking options are just "another stock" which you simply buy low and sell high. Those who jump into their first options trade like this usually get a shock of their lives when they either realize that options don't quite move the way they expect them to move and don't quite behave the way they expect them to behave. Knowing how options work and what their underlying mechanisms are, the logic behind call and put options are the basic knowledge all master options traders need.

Options strategies

The real magic of options trading lies not in simply buying call options for stocks expected to go up or buying put options for stocks expected to go down. The actual magic of options trading lies in the universe of options strategies which allows you to profit not only from an upwards or downwards market but even in a neutral or volatile one. You probably won't be able to learn, practice and master each and every of the hundreds of options strategies but you should have at least one or two options strategies for each class that you are entirely familiar with and have paper traded so that you have a weapon for each market condition.

Technical Analysis

Technical analysis is particularly important for options trading as it is through technical analysis that you can make trend analysis to know what class of options strategy to apply in the first place. Technical analysis is paramount in options trading also due to entry and exit timing which is vital in options trading where there is a fixed expiration. Technical analysis has been used over the decades as a tool for precision entry and exit and is now an important tool in options trading.

Options Greeks

Options Greeks are the mathematical components that define how a particular option would behave in response to factors such as changes in the price of the underlying stock, changes in volatility, changes in interest rate and time decay. An intimate understanding of all the options Greeks allows you to understand better and predict the behavior of an options position. It also allows you to make difficult adjustments to your options position to create a payoff profile that conforms to the exactly predicted behavior of the price of the underlying asset.

Delta Neutral Trading

Delta neutral trading is the ability to tweak a position's delta status to a level that is zero or almost zero such that small volatilities in the price of the underlying asset do not affect the value of the overall position. When delta neutral trading is performed correctly, it could even be used as a hedge which profits no matter which direction the price of the underlying asset breaks out into next. This can only be accomplished by a blend of call options, put options, the underlying asset and even futures. Different situations require a different approach to delta neutral hedging, and that is why it takes a strong knowledge in all of these instruments to do delta neutral trading well.

Mastering all of the above will allow you to realize your dream as a master options trader and be able to make a living from trading options. Are you able to master all of the above?